Old Git Wit

summersdale

OLD GIT WIT

Copyright © Summersdale Publishers Ltd 2006
Illustrations by Roger Roberts

Summersdale Publishers Ltd
46 West Street
Chichester
West Sussex
PO19 1RP
UK

www.summersdale.com

Disclaimer
Every effort has been made to credit all material correctly with reference to copyright material, both illustrative and quoted; should there be any omissions in this respect we apologise and shall be pleased to make the appropriate acknowledgements in any future edition.

Printed in Spain

ISBN: 1-84024-542-5
ISBN 13: 978-1-84024-542-4

Old Git Wit

Contents

Editor's Note

Life expectancy has soared in recent years, with experts telling us that centenarians will soon be as commonplace as two-car households. Old age is here to stay – so put on your specs and pay attention!

However many golden years you've clocked up, or even if you've got it all to look forward to, popular personalities from literature, screen, politics and more share their witty observations on seniority. Typically cynical old grumps including Winston Churchill and Bob Hope moan as only seasoned veterans of life can, while Shakespeare laments an age when one becomes 'blasted with antiquity'. Yet it is good to know that 'Grey Power' is hanging in there to celebrate all that makes elderliness exceptional. Philosopher Bertrand Russell ponders the advantages of white hair while both Picasso and Brigitte Bardot talk of old age as a 'ripening'.

From advice on side-stepping the age question in the Birthdays section to priceless tips in Secrets of Longevity, there are hilarious remarks to sweeten the pill of every aspect of old age. And with contributors ranging from young'uns like Jennifer Saunders and Tom Hanks to the longest-living human being on record, Jeanne Calment (122 at the time of her death), it's worth taking the time to laugh at the wrinkles and forgetfulness.

As Maurice Chevalier so aptly put it, old age is not so bad when you consider the alternative.

Accepting Old Age

When it comes to age
we're all in the same
boat, only some of
us have been aboard
a little longer.

Leo Probst

Old age is not so bad when you consider the alternative.

Maurice Chevalier, French musical-
comedy star (1888–1972)

What's a man's age? He must
hurry more, that's all;
Cram in a day what his youth
took a year to hold.

Robert Browning, British poet (1812–1889)

Old age is like a plane flying through
a storm. Once you're aboard,
there's nothing you can do.

Golda Meir, one of the founders of Israel
and former prime minister (1898–1978)

I guess I don't so much mind being old, as I mind being fat and old.

Peter Gabriel, British pop musician

- - - -

Middle age ends and senescence begins, The day your descendants outnumber your friends.

Ogden Nash, US poet and writer (1902–1971)

Eventually you will reach a point when you stop lying about your age and start bragging about it.

Will Rogers, US comedian and actor (1879–1935)

At my age I do what Mark Twain did. I get my daily paper, look at the obituaries page and if I'm not there I carry on as usual.

Patrick Moore, British astronomer

Getting old is a fascinating thing. The older you get, the older you want to get.

Keith Richards, British rock musician

At middle age the soul should
be opening up like a rose, not
closing up like a cabbage.

John Andrew Holmes, US physician and writer

I always add a year to myself, so I'm
prepared for my next birthday. So
when I was 39, I was already 40.

Nicolas Cage, US actor

Don't let ageing get you down.
It's too hard to get back up.

John Wagner, US-born British comic writer

I'm 59 and people call me middle-aged. How many 118-year-old men do you know?

Barry Cryer, British comedian

Sure I'm for helping the elderly. I'm going to be old myself some day.

Lillian Carter, US social activist and nurse (1898–1983)

Benefits of Old Age

Old age takes away
what we've inherited
and gives us what
we've earned.

Gerald Brenan, British writer (1894–1987)

I have enjoyed greatly the second
blooming that comes when you
finish the life of the emotions and
of personal relations; and suddenly
find – at the age of 50, say – that a
whole new life has opened before
you, filled with things you can think
about, study, or read about... It
is as if a fresh sap of ideas and
thoughts was rising in you.

Agatha Christie, British novelist and
playwright (1890–1976)

One good thing about getting older
is that if you're getting married,
the phrase 'till death do us part'
doesn't sound so horrible. It only
means about 10 or 15 years and
not the eternity it used to mean.

Joy Behar, US comedian and talk show host

We don't grow older, we grow riper.

Pablo Picasso, Spanish painter
and sculptor (1881–1973)

The age of a woman doesn't
mean a thing. The best tunes are
played on the oldest fiddles.

Ralph Waldo Emerson, US writer

It is sad to grow old but nice to ripen.

Brigitte Bardot, French actress and model

❦

Autumn is really the best of the seasons; and I'm not sure that old age isn't the best part of life.

C. S. Lewis, scholar and novelist (1898–1963)

❦

As you grow old, you lose interest in sex, your friends drift away, and your children often ignore you. There are other advantages, of course, but these are the outstanding ones.

Richard Needham, Earl of Kilmorey, former British politician

The more sand has escaped from the hourglass of our life, the clearer we should see through it.

Niccolo Machiavelli, Florentine patriot
and writer (1469–1527)

One of the best parts of growing older? You can flirt all you like since you've become harmless.

Liz Smith, British actress

Old age, believe me, is a good and pleasant thing. It is true you are gently shouldered off the stage, but then you are given such a comfortable front stall as spectator.

Jane Harrison, British classical scholar
and writer (1850–1928)

The great thing about getting
older is that you don't lose all
the other ages you've been.

Madeleine L'Engle, US writer

—◦—

You only have to survive in England
and all is forgiven you... if you can eat
a boiled egg at 90 in England they
think you deserve a Nobel Prize.

Alan Bennett, British writer

—◦—

The great comfort of turning
49 is the realisation that you
are now too old to die young.

Paul Dickson, US writer

I've got cheekier with age. You can get away with murder when you're 71 years old. People just think I'm a silly old fool.

Bernard Manning, British comedian

One of the good things about getting older is you find you're more interesting than most of the people you meet.

Lee Marvin, US actor (1924–1987)

21

In old age we are like a batch
of letters that someone has
sent. We are no longer in
the post, we have arrived.

Knut Hamsun, Norwegian writer (1859–1952)

There's one advantage to being
102. No peer pressure.

Dennis Wolfberg, US comedian (1946–1994)

Eighty's a landmark and people
treat you differently than they
do when you're 79. At 79, if you
drop something it just lies there.
At 80, people pick it up for you.

Helen Van Slyke, writer

The whiter my hair becomes,
the more ready people are
to believe what I say.

Bertrand Russell, British logician and
philosopher (1872–1970)

Old age at least gives me an
excuse for not being very good
at things that I was not very
good at when I was young.

Thomas Sowell, US writer

Birthdays

A diplomat is a
man who always
remembers a woman's
birthday but never
remembers her age.

Robert Frost, US poet (1874–1963)

BIRTHDAYS

You're getting old when the only
thing you want for your birthday
is not to be reminded of it.

Felix Severn

❧

Age is only a number.

Lexi Starling

❧

Birthdays are good for you.
Statistics show that the people
who have the most live the longest.

Father Larry Lorenzoni

❧

When I turned two I was really
anxious, because I'd doubled my
age in a year. I thought, if this keeps
up, by the time I'm six I'll be 90.

Steven Wright, US comedian, actor and writer

My wife hasn't had a birthday
in 4 years. She was born in the
year of our Lord-only-knows.

Unknown

❦

A birthday is just the first day
of another 365-day journey
around the sun. Enjoy the trip.

Unknown

❦

For all the advances in
medicine, there is still no cure
for the common birthday.

John Glenn, US astronaut and politician

Elderly Musings

There are many mysteries in old age but the greatest, surely, is this: in those adverts for walk-in bathtubs, why doesn't all the water gush out when you get in?

Alan Coren, British writer and satirist

And in the end, it's not the
years in your life that count.
It's the life in your years.

Abraham Lincoln, former US president (1809–1865)

About the only thing that comes
to us without effort is old age.

Gloria Pitzer, US cookery writer

When you win, you're an old pro.
When you lose, you're an old man.

Charley Conerly, American football
player (1921–1996)

Life's tragedy is that we get old
too soon and wise too late.

Benjamin Franklin, US diplomat,
politician and printer (1706–1790)

Nobody loves life like him
who is growing old.

Sophocles, Greek tragedian (495–406BC)

One should never make one's debut
in a scandal. One should reserve
that to give interest to one's old age.

Oscar Wilde, Irish poet, novelist
and dramatist (1854–1900)

Oft from shrivelled skin
comes useful counsel.

Saemund, Icelandic priest and scholar (1056–1133)

Life is a moderately good play
with a badly written third act.

Truman Capote, US writer and
playwright (1924–1984)

A lady of a certain age, which means certainly aged.

Lord Byron, Romantic poet and satirist (1788–1824)

Anyone can get old. All you have to do is live long enough.

Groucho Marx, US comedian, actor and singer (1890–1977)

It's true, some wines improve with age. But only if the grapes were good in the first place.

Abigail Van Buren, pen name of US columnist Pauline Phillips and her successor, daughter Jeanne Phillips

Grandchildren don't make a man feel old; it's the knowledge that he's married to a grandmother.

G. Norman Collie

Wisdom doesn't necessarily come with age. Sometimes age just shows up all by itself.

Tom Wilson, US actor, writer and comedian

May you live all the days of your life.

Jonathan Swift, Anglo-Irish writer
and satirist (1667–1745)

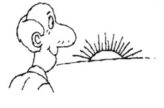

By the time I have money to burn,
my fire will have burnt out.

Unknown

Life can only be understood
backwards, but it must
be lived forwards.

**Soren Kierkegaard, Danish philosopher
and theologian (1813–1855)**

Resolve to be tender with the
young, compassionate with the
aged, sympathetic with the striving,
and tolerant with the weak and
the wrong. Sometime in your life
you will have been all of these.

**Dr Robert H. Goddard, US rocket
engineer (1882–1945)**

Growing old is like being
increasingly penalised for a
crime you haven't committed.

Anthony Powell, British writer (1905–2000)

I go slower as time goes faster.

Mason Cooley, US aphorist (1927–2002)

Half our life is spent trying
to find something to do with
the time we have rushed
through life trying to save.

Will Rogers

Men who are orthodox when they are young are in danger of being middle-aged all their lives.

Walter Lippmann, US writer, journalist and
political commentator (1889–1974)

When I was young, I thought that money was the most important thing in life; now that I am old, I know it is.

Oscar Wilde

Well enough for old folks to rise early, because they have done so many mean things all their lives they can't sleep anyhow.

Mark Twain, US writer (1835–1910)

I don't believe one grows older.
I think that what happens early
on in life is that at a certain age
one stands still and stagnates.

T. S. Eliot, US-born British playwright,
poet and critic (1888–1965)

I am long on ideas, but short
on time. I expect to live to be
only about a hundred.

Thomas Alva Edison, US inventor and
businessman (1847–1931)

Age is something that doesn't
matter, unless you are a cheese.

Billie Burke, US actress (1884–1970)

Old age is the verdict of life.

Amelia E. Barr, English-born US writer
and journalist (1831–1919)

Growing old is something
you do if you're lucky.

Groucho Marx, US comedian

Age wrinkles the body.
Quitting wrinkles the soul.

Douglas MacArthur, US general during
World Wars I and II (1880–1964)

You can't turn back the clock.
But you can wind it up again.

Bonnie Prudden, US rock climber

God gives nuts to those
with no teeth.

Unknown

Old age is life's parody.

Simone de Beauvoir, French
feminist writer (1908–1986)

Life is a funny thing that happens
to you on the way to the grave.

Quentin Crisp, British writer (1908–1999)

Very few people do anything
creative after the age of 35.
The reason is that very few
people do anything creative
before the age of 35.

Joel Hildebrand, US chemist (1881–1983)

Experience, Mistakes and Advice

Experience is a
terrible teacher who
sends horrific bills.

Unknown

For the first half of your life,
people tell you what you should
do; for the second half, they tell
you what you should have done.

Richard Needham

———

I get to be a kid now, because I
wasn't a kid when I was supposed to
be one. But in some ways, I'm like
an old woman – lived it, seen it, done
it, been there, have the T-shirt.

Drew Barrymore, US actress

———

If I had my life to live over again, I'd
make the same mistakes, only sooner.

Tallulah Bankhead, US actress (1902–1968)

If I had my life to live over
again, I'd be a plumber.

Albert Einstein, German-Swiss-American
theoretical physicist (1879–1955)

Age is a high price to
pay for maturity.

Tom Stoppard, British playwright

The man who views the world at
50 the same as he did at 20 has
wasted 30 years of his life.

Muhammad Ali, US boxer

My greatest regret is not knowing at
30 what I knew about women at 60.

Arthur Miller, US playwright and essayist (1915–2005)

I'll never make the mistake
of being 70 again.

Casey Stengel, US baseball player
and manager (1891–1975)

———•———

Autumn is mellower, and
what we lose in flowers, we
more than gain in fruits.

Samuel Butler, British writer and critic (1835–1902)

———•———

Cherish all your happy moments:
they make a fine cushion for old age.

Christopher Morley, US journalist,
novelist and poet (1890–1957)

I used to have a sign over my computer that read 'Old dogs can learn new tricks', but lately I sometimes ask myself how many more new tricks I want to learn. Wouldn't it just be easier to be outdated?

Ram Dass, US professor of psychology, researcher and writer

You don't appreciate a lot of stuff in school until you get older. Little things like being spanked every day by a middle-aged woman: stuff you pay good money for in later life.

Emo Philips, US comedian

Whenever I get down about life going by too quickly, what helps me is a little mantra that I repeat to myself: at least I'm not a fruit fly.

Ray Romano, US comedian and actor

We learn from experience that men never learn anything from experience.

George Bernard Shaw, Irish literary critic, playwright and 1925 Nobel Prize Winner for Literature (1856–1950)

The post office has a great charm at one point of our lives. When you have lived to my age you will begin to think letters are never worth going through the rain for.

Jane Austen, British novelist and writer (1775–1817)

A prune is an experienced plum.

John Trattner, former US diplomat, writer and journalist

I have lived in the world just long enough to look carefully the second time into those things that I am most certain of the first time.

Josh Billings, US writer and lecturer (1818–1885)

I advise you to go on living solely to enrage those who are paying your annuities. It is the only pleasure I have left.

François Voltaire, French philosopher and writer (1694–1778)

When I was young, I was told:
'You'll see when you're 50.' I'm
50 and I haven't seen a thing.

Erik Satie, French composer and pianist (1866–1925)

When people tell you how
young you look, they are also
telling you how old you are.

Cary Grant, English-born US actor (1904–1986)

Life is too short to learn German.

Richard Porson, British classical scholar (1759–1808)

Just remember, once you're over
the hill, you begin to pick up speed.

Charles M. Schulz, US cartoonist (1922–2000)

As I grow older, I pay less
attention to what men say. I
just watch what they do.

Andrew Carnegie, Scottish-born US industrialist
and philanthropist (1835–1919)

Experience is a comb life gives
you after you lose your hair.

Judith Stern, writer (1829–1868)

The time to begin most
things is ten years ago.

Mignon McLaughlin, US journalist
and author (1913–1983)

The Good
Old Days

Most people like the
old days best – they
were younger then.

Unknown

Nothing is more responsible for the good old days than a bad memory.

Franklin Pierce Adams, US writer (1881–1960)

Ⓧ

It becomes increasingly easy, as you get older, to drown in nostalgia.

Ted Koppel, US journalist

Ⓧ

Sometimes when a man recalls the good old days, he's really thinking of his bad young days.

Unknown

Growing Old Gracefully

When it comes to staying young, a mind-lift beats a face-lift any day.

Marty Bucella, cartoonist

Age should not have its face lifted, but it should rather teach the world to admire wrinkles as the etching of experience and the firm line of character.

Clarence Day, US writer (1874–1935)

Don't retouch my wrinkles in the photograph. I would not want it to be thought that I had lived for all these years without having anything to show for it.

The Queen Mother (1900–2002)

Let us respect grey hairs,
especially our own.

J. P. Sears

The best mirror is an old friend.

George Herbert, British poet and
clergyman (1593–1633)

I'd like to grow very old as
slowly as possible.

Irene Mayer Selznick, US theatrical
producer (1907–1990)

How foolish to think that one can
ever slam the door in the face of age.
Much wiser to be polite and gracious
and ask him to lunch in advance.

Noël Coward, British actor, composer
and playwright (1899–1973)

A woman past 40 should
make up her mind to be
young, and not her face.

Billie Burke

Time may be a great healer,
but it's a lousy beautician.

Unknown

I don't plan to grow old
gracefully; I plan to have
facelifts until my ears meet.

Rita Rudner, US writer and comedienne

The easiest way to diminish
the appearance of wrinkles
is to keep your glasses off
when you look in the mirror.

Joan Rivers, US comedienne

Beautiful young people are
accidents of nature, but beautiful
old people are works of art.

Eleanor Roosevelt, former US First Lady (1884–1962)

The only real way to look younger
is not to be born so soon.

Charles M. Schulz

Grumpiness

There is absolutely
nothing to be said in
favour of growing old.
There ought to be
legislation against it.

Patrick Moore

The older a man gets, the farther he had to walk to school as a boy.

Henry Brightman

—◆—

The older you get the stronger the wind gets – and it's always in your face.

Jack Nicklaus, former US golfer

—◆—

I refused to go on that *Grumpy Old Men* programme because I said, 'If I go on, I will be grumpy about grumpy old men.'

Stephen Fry, British comedian, actor and writer

Some grow bitter with age;
the more their teeth drop out,
the more biting they get.

George D. Prentice, US newspaper
editor and writer (1802–1870)

There's no law that decrees when
not to whinge, but you reach a
certain age – 80 seems about right
– when you're expected to manifest
querulousness – the coffee's too
hot, the boiled egg's too soft...

Clement Freud, British writer,
broadcaster and politician

My Uncle Sammy was an
angry man. He had printed
on his tombstone: 'What
are you looking at?'

Margaret Smith, US comedienne

If old people were to mobilise en
masse they would constitute a
formidable fighting force, as anyone
who has ever had the temerity to try
to board a bus ahead of a little old
lady with an umbrella well knows.

Vera Forrester

Health and Exercise

Exercise daily. Eat
wisely. Die anyway.

Unknown

At my age getting a second doctor's opinion is kinda like switching slot machines.

Jimmy Carter, former US president

———

To win back my youth... there is nothing I wouldn't do – except take exercise, get up early, or be a useful member of the community.

Oscar Wilde

———

The denunciation of the young is a necessary part of the hygiene of older people, and greatly assists in the circulation of their blood.

Logan Pearsall Smith, US essayist and critic (1865–1946), Afterthoughts

FLICK

If I'm feeling really wild I don't
floss before bedtime.

Judith Viorst, US writer

—————

People who say you're just as old as
you feel are all wrong, fortunately.

Russell Baker, US writer

I'd like to learn to ski but I'm 44 and I'm worried about my knees. They creak a lot and I'm afraid they might start an avalanche.

Jonathan Ross, British comedian and
television and radio presenter

When I was 40, my doctor advised me that a man in his 40s shouldn't play tennis. I heeded his advice carefully and could hardly wait until I reached 50 to start again.

Hugo L. Black, US jurist, lawyer
and politician (1886–1971)

I am getting to an age when I can only enjoy the last sport left. It is called hunting for your spectacles.

Sir Edward Grey, politician and
ornithologist (1862–1933)

Old people should not eat
health foods. They need all the
preservatives they can get.

Robert Orben, US magician and comedy writer

———•———

I've just become a pensioner
so I've started saving up for
my own hospital trolley.

Tom Baker, British actor

———•———

If, at the age of 30, you are stiff
and out of shape, then you are
old. If, at 60, you are supple and
strong, then you are young.

Joseph Pilates, Greek-German inventor of the
Pilates physical fitness method (1880–1967)

If you rest, you rust.

Helen Hayes, US stage and film actress (1900–1993)

———— ◦ ————

Middle age is when you
are not inclined to exercise
anything but caution.

Arthur Murray, US dance instructor
and businessman (1895–1991)

———— ◦ ————

You can't be as old as I am without
waking up with a surprised look
on your face every morning: 'Holy
Christ, what da ya know – I'm still
around!' It's absolutely amazing that
I survived all the booze and smoking
and the cars and the career.

Paul Newman, US actor

Each year it grows harder to make ends meet – the ends I refer to are hands and feet.

Richard Armour, US poet and author (1906–1989)

I don't want a flu jab. I like getting flu. It gives me something else to complain about.

David Letterman, US television talk show host

One of the advantages of
being 70 is that you need only
4 hours' sleep. True, you need
it 4 times a day, but still.

**Denis Norden, British comedy writer
and television presenter**

I keep fit. Every morning,
I do a hundred laps of an
Olympic-sized swimming pool
– in a small motor launch.

Peter Cook, British actor and comedian (1937–1995)

Now I'm getting older I take health
supplements: geranium, dandelion,
passionflower, hibiscus. I feel
great, and when I pee, I experience
the fresh scent of potpourri.

Sheila Wenz, US comedienne

As for me, except for an
occasional heart attack, I feel
as young as I ever did.

Robert Benchley, US actor and writer (1889–1945)

Now I'm over 50 my doctor says I
should go out and get more fresh
air and exercise. I said, 'All right, I'll
drive with the car window open.'

Angus Walker

When you get to my age life
seems little more than one long
march to and from the lavatory.

John Mortimer, British writer

If I'd known I was gonna live this long,
I'd have taken better care of myself.

Eubie Blake, US pianist and composer
of ragtime music (1887–1983)

My mother is no spring chicken
although she has got as many
chemicals in her as one.

Dame Edna Everage, alter ego of
Australian comedian Barry Humphries

I'm 43, and for the first time this
year I have felt older. I'm slowly
becoming more decrepit. I think
you just move to the country
and wear an old fleece.

Jennifer Saunders, British comedienne

How Old?

The older I get,
the older old is.

Tom Baker, British actor

How Old?

Old age is always 15 years
older than what I am.

Bernard Baruch, US economist and adviser
to US presidents (1870–1965)

I do wish I could tell you my
age but it's impossible. It
keeps changing all the time.

Greer Garson, British actress (1908–1996)

I believe in loyalty; I think when
a woman reaches an age she
likes she should stick to it.

Eva Gabor, Hungarian-born US actress
and entertainer (1921–1995)

Professionally, I have no age.

Kathleen Turner, US actress

I'm as old as my tongue and a little bit older than my teeth.

Kris Kringle, Miracle on 34th Street

I'm 60 years of age. That's 16 Celsius.

George Carlin, US stand-up comedian, actor and writer

I am just turning 40 and taking my time about it.

Harold Lloyd, US actor and film-maker at age 77 (1893–1971)

I was born in 1962. True. And the room next to me was 1963.

Joan Rivers

I refuse to admit that I am more
than 52, even if that makes
my children illegitimate.

Nancy Astor, US-born politician and first woman to
sit in the British House of Commons (1879–1964)

Age is a number – mine is unlisted.

Unknown

I'm not 40, I'm 18 with 22
years experience.

Unknown

Whenever the talk turns to age,
I say I am 49 plus VAT.

Lionel Blair, British dancer and television presenter

We're obsessed with age. Numbers are always and pointlessly attached to every name that's published in a newspaper: 'Joe Creamer, 43, and his daughter, Tiffany-Ann, 9, were merrily chasing a bunny, 2, when Tiffany-Ann tripped on the root of a tree, 106.'

Joan Rivers

She may very well pass for 43 in the dusk with the light behind her!

W. S. Gilbert, British dramatist and librettist (1836–1911)

No woman should ever be quite accurate about her age. It looks so calculating.

Oscar Wilde

I don't know how old I am
because the goat ate the Bible
that had my birth certificate in
it. The goat lived to be 27.

Satchel Paige

·

I still think of myself as I was
25 years ago. Then I look
in the mirror and see an old
bastard and I realise it's me.

Dave Allen, Irish comedian

·

First women subtract from their
age, then they divide it, and then
they extract its square root.

Unknown

I'm 65 and I guess that puts me in with the geriatrics. But if there were 15 months in every year, I'd only be 48. That's the trouble with us. We number everything. Take women, for example. I think they deserve to have more than 12 years between the ages of 28 and 40.

James Thurber, US writer and cartoonist (1894–1961)

Immortality

Millions long for immortality who do not know what to do with themselves on a rainy Sunday afternoon.

Susan Ertz, British writer (1894–1985)

OLD GIT WIT

He had decided to live forever
or die in the attempt.

Joseph Heller, US writer (1923–1999)

The first step to eternal
life is you have to die.

Chuck Palahniuk, US journalist

There's nothing wrong with you
that reincarnation won't cure.

Jack E. Leonard, US comedian (1910–1973)

The only thing wrong with
immortality is that it tends
to go on forever.

Herb Caen, US journalist (1916–1997)

I don't want to achieve immortality
through my work, I want to
achieve it through not dying.

Woody Allen, US actor, writer and film director

If you live to be one hundred,
you've got it made. Very few
people die past that age.

George Burns, US comedian and actor (1896–1996)

I intend to live forever.
So far, so good.

Stephen Wright, US writer

Memory Loss

As you get older
three things happen.
The first is your
memory goes, and
I can't remember
the other two...

Norman Wisdom, British comedian and actor

I believe the true function of age is memory. I'm recording as fast as I can.

Rita Mae Brown, US writer and social activist

❖

Once you've accumulated sufficient knowledge to get by, you're too old to remember it.

Unknown

❖

They will all have heard that story of yours before – but if you tell it well they won't mind hearing it again.

Thora Hird, British actress (1911–2003)

❖

After the age of 80, everything reminds you of something else.

Lowell Thomas, US writer, broadcaster and traveller (1892–1981)

Interviewer: Can you remember
any of your past lives?
The Dalai Lama: At my age I have
a problem remembering what
happened yesterday.

By the time you're 80 years
old you've learned everything.
You only have to remember it.

George Burns

Middle Age

Middle age is the awkward period when Father Time starts catching up with Mother Nature.

Harold Coffin, US journalist (1905–1981)

Middle age is when, whenever you go on holiday, you pack a sweater.

Denis Norden

❦

It's hard to feel middle-aged, because how can you tell how long you are going to live?

Mignon McLaughlin

❦

Middle age is when your broad mind and narrow waist begin to change places.

E. Joseph Cossman, US entrepreneur (1918–2002)

❦

Middle age is when you're old enough to know better but still young enough to do it.

Ogden Nash

Middle age is the time when a man is always thinking that in a week or two he will feel as good as ever.

Don Marquis, US columnist, novelist,
playwright and poet, (1878–1937)

Years ago we discovered the exact point, the dead centre of middle age. It occurs when you are too young to take up golf and too old to rush to the net.

Franklin Adams, US journalist, columnist
and translator (1881–1960)

Middle age is when work is a lot less fun, and fun is a lot more work.

Milton Berle, US comedian and actor (1908–2002)

Setting a good example for
your children takes all the
fun out of middle age.

William Feather, US writer and publisher (1889–1981)

Middle Age: When you
begin to exchange your
emotions for symptoms.

Georges Clemenceau, French doctor
and journalist (1841–1929)

Middle age is when your classmates
are so grey and wrinkled and
bald they don't recognise you.

Bennett Cerf, founder of Random House (1898–1971)

Middle age is the time in life
when, after pulling in your
stomach, you look as if you
ought to pull in your stomach.

Unknown

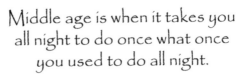

Middle age is when it takes you
all night to do once what once
you used to do all night.

Kenny Everett, British radio DJ and
television entertainer (1944–1995)

The enemy of society is middle class
and the enemy of life is middle age.

Orson Welles, US actor, director,
producer and writer (1915–1985)

Middle age is when everything new
you feel is likely to be a symptom.

Dr Laurence J. Peter, Canadian hierarchiologist
and educator (1919–1990)

Spiritual sloth, or acedia, was known
as The Sin of the Middle Ages.
It's the sin of my middle age, too.

Mignon McLaughlin

The long, dull, monotonous years
of middle-aged prosperity or
middle-aged adversity are excellent
campaigning weather for the devil.

C. S. Lewis

You know you've reached middle
age when your weightlifting
consists merely of standing up.

Bob Hope, English-born US actor
and comedian (1903–2003)

Mid-life crisis is that moment when
you realise your children and your
clothes are about the same age.

William D. Tammeus, US columnist

Middle age is when you're
sitting at home on a Saturday
night and the telephone rings
and you hope it isn't for you.

Ogden Nash

Middle age is when your age starts
to show around your middle.

Bob Hope

Middle Age – later than you think
and sooner than you expect.

Earl Wilson, baseball player (1934–2005)

The really frightening thing about
middle age is the knowledge
that you'll grow out of it.

Doris Day, US actress and singer

If you want to recapture your
youth, just cut off his allowance.

Al Bernstein, US writer and entertainer

Middle age is when you choose your cereal for the fibre, not the toy.

Unknown

Middle age is when you're faced with two temptations and you choose the one that will get you home by nine o'clock.

Ronald Reagan, former US president (1911–2004)

Nature of Old Age

The first 40 years of life give us the text: the next 30 supply the commentary.

Arthur Schopenhauer, German
philosopher (1788–1860)

As we grow older, our bodies get shorter and our anecdotes longer.

Robert Quillen, US humorist, journalist
and cartoonist (1887–1948)

You know you've grown up when you become obsessed with the thermostat.

Jeff Foxworthy, US comedian and actor

As one grows older, one becomes wiser and more foolish.

François de La Rochefoucauld, classical writer,
leading exponent of the Maxime (1613–1680)

Old age means realising you will
never own all the dogs you wanted to.

Joe Gores, US writer

An old man looks permanent, as
if he had been born an old man.

H. E. Bates, British writer

Old age is when you resent
the swimsuit issue of *Sports
Illustrated* because there are
fewer articles to read.

George Burns

❧

Time and trouble will tame
an advanced young woman,
but an advanced old woman is
uncontrollable by any earthly force.

Dorothy L. Sayers, British writer (1893–1957)

❧

Forty is the old age of youth;
fifty is the youth of old age.

French proverb

Growing old is no more than
a bad habit, which a busy
person has no time to form.

**Andre Maurois, French biographer,
novelist and essayist (1885–1967)**

Age seldom arrives smoothly
or quickly. It's more often
a succession of jerks.

Jean Rhys, Caribbean novelist (1894–1979)

The essence of age is intellect.
Wherever that appears, we call it old.

Ralph Waldo Emerson

Not Growing Up

It takes a long time
to grow young.

Pablo Picasso

Life would be infinitely happier if
we could only be born at the age
of 80 and gradually approach 18.

Mark Twain

Age does not diminish the extreme
disappointment of having a scoop
of ice cream fall from the cone.

Jim Fiebig

The surprising thing about
young fools is how many
survive to become old fools.

Doug Larson, US columnist

The older you get the more
important it is not to act your age.

Ashleigh Brilliant, British-born US writer and cartoonist

Growing old is compulsory,
growing up is optional.

Bob Monkhouse, British comedian (1928–2003)

You're only young once, but
you can be immature forever.

John Greier

The secret of genius is to carry the
spirit of the child into old age, which
means never losing your enthusiasm.

Aldous Huxley, British writer (1894–1963)

Almost all my middle-aged and
elderly acquaintances, including me,
feel about 25, unless we haven't had
our coffee, in which case we feel 107.

Martha Beck, US sociologist and writer

The tragedy of old age is not that
one is old, but that one is young.

Oscar Wilde

I've got to go and see the old folk.

The Queen Mother at age 97, spotting a group
of pensioners at Cheltenham Racecourse

Inside every older person is
a younger person wondering
what the hell happened.

Cora Harvey Armstrong

I plan on growing old much later
in life, or maybe not at all.

Patty Carey

❦

Fifty is the new 34.

Tom Hanks, US actor

❦

Few people know how to be old.

Maggie Kuhn, US social activist (1905–1995)

When they tell me I'm too old to do something, I attempt it immediately.

Pablo Picasso

Pleasures of Old Age

W. C. Fields has a profound respect for old age. Especially when it's bottled.

Gene Fowler, US author, journalist and dramatist (1890–1960)

My grandmother is over 80
and still doesn't need glasses.
Drinks right out of the bottle.

Henry Youngman, English-born US
comedian and violinist (1906–1998)

✦

You know you're getting old
when a four-letter word for
something pleasurable two people
can do in bed is R-E-A-D.

Denis Norden

✦

When you get to 52 food becomes
more important than sex.

Prue Leith, South Aftrican-born British
broadcaster and cookery writer

One of the many pleasures of old age is giving things up.

Malcolm Muggeridge, British journalist and author (1903–1990)

I smoke 10 to 15 cigars a day, at my age I have to hold on to something.

George Burns

Jameson's Irish Whiskey really does improve with age: the older I get the more I like it.

Bob Monkhouse

I'm at the age where food has
taken the place of sex in my
life. In fact, I've just had a mirror
put over my kitchen table.

Rodney Dangerfield, US comedian
and actor (1921–2004)

I always make a point of starting
the day at 6 a.m. with champagne.
It goes straight to the heart and
cheers one up. White wine won't
do. You need the bubbles.

John Mortimer

Physical Effects

You don't know real embarrassment until your hip sets off a metal detector.

Ross McGuinness

You know you're getting old when everything hurts. And what doesn't hurt doesn't work.

Hy Gardner, US columnist (1908–1989)

Have you not a moist eye, a dry hand, a yellow cheek, a white beard, a decreasing leg, an increasing belly? Is not your voice broken, your wind short, your chin double, your wit single, and every part about you blasted with antiquity?

William Shakespeare, English poet and playwright (1564–1616)

I don't want to end up in an old folk's home wearing incompetence pads. I'm still compost mentis.

Harriet Wynn

Many of us are at the 'metallic' age – gold in our teeth, silver in our hair, and lead in our pants.

Unknown

———◆———

Advanced old age is when you sit in a rocking chair and can't get it going.

Eliakim Katz, Canadian professor of economics

———◆———

They say that age is all in your mind. The trick is keeping it from creeping down into your body.

Unknown

———◆———

I don't need you to remind me of my age, I have a bladder to do that for me.

Stephen Fry

I knew I was going bald when
it was taking longer and
longer to wash my face.

Harry Hill, British comedian

Life begins at 40 – but so do fallen
arches, rheumatism, faulty eyesight,
and the tendency to tell a story to
the same person three or four times.

Helen Rowland, English-American writer (1876–1950)

It's been said that if you're not radical at 20, you have no heart; if you're still radical at 40, you have no brain. Of course, either way, at 60 you usually have no teeth.

Bill Maher, US comedian, actor, writer and producer

Everything slows down with age, except the time it takes cake and ice cream to reach your hips.

John Wagner

My friend George has false teeth – with braces on them.

Steven Wright

I don't feel 80. In fact I don't
feel anything until noon,
then it's time for my nap.

Bob Hope

They talk about the economy
this year. Hey, my hairline is in
recession, my waistline is in inflation.
Altogether, I'm in a depression.

Rick Majerus

It's extraordinary. My mother
doesn't need glasses at all and
here I am at 52, 56 – well, whatever
age I am – and can't see a thing.

Queen Elizabeth II

Wrinkles should merely indicate
where smiles have been.

Mark Twain

35 is when you finally get
your head together and your
body starts falling apart.

Caryn Leschen, US graphic artist and copywriter

My grandma told me, 'The good news is, after menopause the hair on your legs gets really thin and you don't have to shave any more. Which is great because it means you have more time to work on your new moustache.'

Karen Haber, US writer

Robert Redford used to be such a handsome man and now look at him: everything has dropped, expanded and turned a funny colour.

George Best, Irish football player (1946–2005)

After a certain number of years our faces become our biographies.

Cynthia Ozick, US writer

I have the body of an 18 year-
old. I keep it in the fridge.

Spike Milligan, British comedian (1918–2002)

Thoughtfulness begets wrinkles.

Charles Dickens, British novelist (1812–1870)

I had a job selling hearing aids from
door to door. It wasn't easy, because
your best prospects never answered.

Bob Monkhouse

Beauty and ugliness disappear
equally under the wrinkles of age;
one is lost in them, the other hidden.

Jonathan Petit Senn, French poet (1792–1870)

Like a lot of fellows around here,
I have a furniture problem. My
chest has fallen into my drawers.

Billy Casper, US golfer

At 75, I sleep like a log. I never
have to get up in the middle of the
night to go to the bathroom. I go
in the morning. Every morning,
like clockwork, at 7 a.m., I pee.
Unfortunately, I don't wake up till 8.

Harry Beckworth

Alas, after a certain age every
man is responsible for his face.

Albert Camus, novelist, essayist, playwright and
1957 Nobel Prize Winner for Literature (1913–1960)

I'm at an age where my back
goes out more than I do.

Phyllis Diller, US comedian

Grey hair is God's graffiti.

Bill Cosby, US actor, comedian and producer

I used to think I'd like less grey
hair. Now I'd like more of it.

Richie Benaud, former Australian cricketer

I recently had my
annual physical
examination, which I
get once every seven
years, and when the
nurse weighed me,
I was shocked to
discover how much
stronger the Earth's
gravitational pull has
become since 1990.

Dave Barry, US writer and comedian

Retirement

People ought to retire at 40 when they feel over-used and go back to work at 65 when they feel useless.

Sister Carol Anne O'Marie, US nun and writer

Retired is being tired twice... first tired of working, then tired of not.

Richard Armour

Δ

It's very hard to make a home for a man if he's always in it.

Winifred Kirkland, US writer (1872–1943)

Δ

I don't want to retire. I'm not that good at crossword puzzles.

Norman Mailer, US writer

Δ

When men reach their sixties and retire, they go to pieces. Women go right on cooking.

Gail Sheehy, US writer

My parents live in a retirement
community, which is basically
a minimum-security prison
with a golf course.

Joel Warshaw

＊

When a man retires his wife
gets twice the husband but
only half the income.

Chi Chi Rodriguez, former Puerto Rican golfer

＊

When a man falls into his
anecdotage, it is a sign for him
to retire from the world.

Benjamin Disraeli, 1st Earl of Beaconsfield, former
British prime minister and literary figure (1804–1881)

We spend our lives on the run: we get up by the clock, eat and sleep by the clock, get up again, go to work – and then we retire. And what do they give us? A bloody clock.

Dave Allen

The best time to start thinking about your retirement is before the boss does.

Unknown

Don't retire, retread!

Robert Otterbourg, US writer

———•———

The trouble with retirement is that you never get a day off.

Abe Lemons, basketball coach (1922–2002)

———•———

I'm 42 around the chest, 52 around the waist, 92 around the golf course and a nuisance around the house.

Groucho Marx

———•———

Once it was impossible to find any Bond villains older than myself, I retired.

Roger Moore, British actor

Secrets of Longevity

You can live to be a
hundred if you give
up all the things that
make you want to live
to be a hundred.

Woody Allen

The secret of staying young
is to live honestly, eat slowly
and lie about your age.

Lucille Ball, US actress and comedienne (1911–1989)

❖

I've found a formula for avoiding
these exaggerated fears of age;
you take care of every day – let the
calendar take care of the years.

Ed Wynn, US actor (1886–1966)

❖

Interviewer: 'You've reached the ripe
old age of 121. What do you
expect the future will be like?'
'Very short.'

Jeanne Calment (1875–1997)

Every one desires to live long,
but no one would be old.

Jonathan Swift

My first advice on how not to
grow old would be to choose
your ancestors carefully.

Bertrand Russell

The fountain of youth is a
mixture of gin and vermouth.

Cole Porter, US composer and
songwriter (1891–1964)

Old age is like everything
else. To make a success of it,
you've got to start young.

Theodore Roosevelt, former US
president (1858–1919)

The trick is growing up
without growing old.

Casey Stengel

It's a good idea to obey all the
rules when you're young just
so you'll have the strength to
break them when you're old.

Mark Twain

Ageing seems to be the only
available way to live a long life.

Daniel Francois Esprit Auber, French
composer (1782–1871)

A man 90 years old was asked to what he attributed his longevity. I reckon, he said, with a twinkle in his eye, it's because most nights I went to bed and slept when I should have sat up and worried.

Dorothea Kent, US actress (1916–1990)

Age is getting to know all the ways the world turns, so that if you cannot turn the world the way you want, you can at least get out of the way so you won't get run over.

Miriam Makeba, South African singer

The idea is to die young as late as possible.

Ashley Montagu, British anthropologist and humanist (1905–1999)

A man's only as old as
the woman he feels.

Groucho Marx

I'll tell ya how to stay young:
Hang around with older people.

Bob Hope

Age is a question of mind
over matter. If you don't
mind, it doesn't matter!

Mark Twain

❖

Since people are going to
be living longer and getting
older, they'll just have to learn
how to be babies longer.

Andy Warhol, US artist (1928–1987)

❖

The great secret that all old
people share is that you really
haven't changed in 70 or 80 years.
Your body changes, but you
don't change at all. And that, of
course, causes great confusion.

Doris Lessing, British writer

To stop ageing – keep on raging.

Michael Forbes, US politician

More people would live to a
ripe old age if they weren't
too busy providing for it.

Unknown

I can only assume that it is largely
due to the accumulation of toasts
to my health over the years that I
am still enjoying a fairly satisfactory
state of health and have reached
such an unexpectedly great age.

Prince Philip, The Duke of Edinburgh

———•———

Old age is no place for sissies.

Bette Davis, US actress (1908–1989)

Senility

They tell you that
you'll lose your mind
when you grow older.
What they don't tell
you is that you won't
miss it very much.

Malcolm Cowley, US critic, writer and editor
of The New Republic (1898–1989)

I am in the prime of senility.

Benjamin Franklin

—◆—

How the hell should I know?
Most of the people my age are
dead. You could look it up.

Casey Stengel

—◆—

When you become senile,
you won't know it.

Bill Cosby

When I was young I was called
a rugged individualist. When I
was in my fifties I was considered
eccentric. Here I am doing and
saying the same things I did
then and I'm labelled senile.

George Burns

They say that after the age of 20
you lose 50,000 brain cells a day. I
don't believe it. I think it's much more.

Ned Sherrin, British broadcaster,
writer and stage director

My experience is that as soon
as people are old enough
to know better, they don't
know anything at all.

Oscar Wilde

Sex and Indecency

Old age is an excellent time for outrage. My goal is to say or do at least one outrageous thing every week.

Maggie Kuhn

A medical report states that the human male is physically capable of enjoying sex up to and even beyond the age of 80. Not as a participant, of course...

Denis Norden

Don't worry about temptation as you grow older, it starts avoiding you.

Winston Churchill, former British prime minister (1874–1965)

I've always thought that the stereotype of the dirty old man is really the creation of a dirty young man who wants the field to himself.

Hugh Downs, US television host, producer and writer

Sex manual for the more mature – 'How to tell an orgasm from a heart attack!'

Unknown

I can still enjoy sex at 75. I live at 76, so it's no distance.

Bob Monkhouse

The older one grows, the more one likes indecency.

Virginia Woolf, British writer (1882–1941)

I'm 78 but I still use a condom when I have sex. I can't take the damp.

Alan Gregory

I suspect most self-described 18-year-old Scandinavian women named Inga who collect and wear string bikinis are, in reality, more likely to be middle-aged, pot-bellied guys named Lou who collect and wear string cheese.

Pat Sajak, US television host

After being told his
flies were undone:
No matter. The dead bird
does not fall out of the nest.

Winston Churchill

Middle age is when a guy keeps
turning off the lights for economical
rather then romantic reasons.

Lillian Carter

What most persons consider
as virtue, after the age of 40
is simply a loss of energy.

François Voltaire

After a man passes 60, his mischief is mainly in his head.

Edgar Watson Howe, US editor
and writer (1853–1937)

There is no pleasure worth forgoing just for an extra three years in the geriatric ward.

John Mortimer

Now that I'm 78, I do Tantric sex because it's very slow. My favourite position is called the plumber. You stay in all day but nobody comes.

John Mortimer

❧—◆—❧

Talk about getting old. I was getting dressed and a peeping tom looked in the window, took a look and pulled down the shade.

Joan Rivers

❧—◆—❧

Old age likes indecency.
It's a sign of life.

Mason Cooley

Of all the faculties, the last to leave us is sexual desire. That means that long after wearing bifocals and hearing aids, we'll still be making love. We just won't know with whom.

Jack Paar, US radio and television
talk show host (1918–2004)

Signs of Old Age

They say the first
thing to go when
you're old is your
legs or your eyesight.
It isn't true. The
first thing to go is
parallel parking.

Kurt Vonnegut, US novelist, satirist and graphic artist

You know you're old if they have
discontinued your blood type.

Phyllis Diller

———

The ageing process has you
firmly in its grasp if you never get
the urge to throw a snowball.

Doug Larson

———

It's a sign of age if you feel like
the morning after the night before
and you haven't been anywhere.

Unknown

Grandmother, as she gets older,
is not fading, but becoming
more concentrated.

Paulette Alden, US writer

You're an old-timer if you can
remember when setting the world
on fire was a figure of speech.

Franklin P. Jones, US businessman (1887–1929)

Old age is when the liver spots
show through your gloves.

Phyllis Diller

One day you look in the mirror
and realise the face you are
shaving is your father's.

Robert Harris, British writer

One of the signs of old age is that
you have to carry your senses
around in your handbag – glasses,
hearing aids, dentures etc.

Kurt Strauss, US actor and voice actor

You know you are getting old when
the candles cost more than the cake.

Bob Hope

A man loses his illusions first, his
teeth second, and his follies last.

Helen Rowland

Old age comes on suddenly, and not gradually as is first thought.

Emily Dickinson, US poet (1830–1886)

I'm getting on. I'm now equipped with a snooze button.

Denis Norden

There is only one cure for grey. It was invented by a Frenchman. It is called the guillotine.

P. G. Wodehouse, British writer (1881–1975)

You know you're getting old when your idea of a hot, flaming desire is a barbecued steak.

Victoria Fabiano

You know you're getting older
when the first thing you do
after you're done eating is
look for a place to lie down.

Louie Anderson, US comedian, writer and actor

———•—•———

You know you're getting old
when you look at a beautiful
19-year-old girl and you find
yourself thinking, 'Gee, I wonder
what her mother looks like.'

Unknown

———•—•———

Inflation is when you pay
fifteen dollars for the ten-dollar
haircut you used to get for five
dollars when you had hair.

Sam Ewing, US writer (1921–2001)

The first sign of maturity is
the discovery that the volume
knob also turns to the left.

Jerry M. Wright

First, you forget names, then you
forget faces. Next, you forget
to pull your zipper up and finally
you forget to pull it down.

Leo Rosenberg

You know you're getting old
when all the names in your black
book have M.D. after them.

Arnold Palmer, US golfer

You're not old until it takes
you longer to rest up than
it does to get tired.

Phog Allen, US basketball coach (1885–1974)

You know you're getting older if you
have more fingers than real teeth.

Rodney Dangerfield

153

Style

If you really want to annoy your glamorous, well-preserved 42-year-old auntie, say, 'I bet you were really pretty when you were young.'

Lily Savage, alter ego of British comedian and television presenter Paul O'Grady

My dad's pants kept creeping
up on him. By 65 he was just
a pair of pants and a head.

Jeff Altman, US comedian

❧

Age becomes reality when you
hear someone refer to 'that
attractive young woman standing
next to the woman in the green
dress,' and you find that you're
the one in the green dress.

Lois Wyse, US writer

❧

You know you're getting old when
you're dashing through Marks
and Spencer's, spot a pair of
Dr Scholl's sandals, stop, and
think, hmm, they look comfy.

Victoria Wood, British comedienne, actress and writer

Talking 'bout the Generations

It's hard for me to get used to these changing times. I can remember when the air was clean and sex was dirty.

George Burns

My generation thought 'fast food' was something you ate during Lent, a 'Big Mac' was an oversized raincoat and 'crumpet' was something you had for tea. 'Sheltered accommodation' was a place where you waited for a bus, 'time-sharing' meant togetherness and you kept 'coke' in the coal house.

Joan Collins, British actress

At the age of 20, we don't care what the world thinks of us; at 30 we worry about what it is thinking of us; at 40, we discover that it wasn't thinking of us at all.

Unknown

There are three periods in
life: youth, middle age and
'how well you look'.

Nelson Rockefeller, former US vice president
and governor of New York (1908–1979)

❧—◆—☙

Girls used to come up to me
and say, 'My sister loves you.'
Now girls come up to me and
say, 'My mother loves you.'

Lee Mazzilli, US baseball player

❧—◆—☙

Youth is the time of getting,
middle age of improving, and
old age of spending.

Anne Bradstreet, US poet (1612–1672)

Parents often talk about the younger generation as if they didn't have anything to do with it.

Dr. Haim Ginott, psychologist and writer (1922– 1973)

Wrinkles are hereditary. Parents get them from their children.

Doris Day

At 16 I was stupid, confused and indecisive. At 25 I was wise, self-confident, prepossessing and assertive. At 45 I am stupid, confused, insecure and indecisive. Who would have supposed that maturity is only a short break in adolescence?

Jules Feiffer, US cartoonist and writer

Young people tell what they are doing, old people what they have done and fools what they wish to do.

French proverb

Why do grandparents and grandchildren get along so well? They have the same enemy – the mother.

Claudette Colbert, French-born US stage and film actress (1903–1996)

When you are about 35 years old, something terrible always happens to music.

Steve Race, British pianist, composer and radio disc jockey

There are three stages in an actor's career: Who is John Amos? Get me John Amos. Get me a young John Amos.

John Amos, US actor

There are only three ages for women in Hollywood – Babe, District Attorney, and Driving Miss Daisy.

Goldie Hawn, US actress

My nan said, 'What do you mean when you say the computer went down on you?'

Joseph Longthorne

There are three stages of man:
he believes in Santa Claus;
he does not believe in Santa
Claus; he is Santa Claus.

Bob Phillips, US writer

At 20 years of age the will reigns;
at 30 the wit; at 40 the judgement.

Benjamin Franklin

In case you're worried about
what's going to become of the
younger generation, it's going
to grow up and start worrying
about the younger generation.

Roger Allen, US writer

No matter how old a mother is
she watches her middle-aged
children for signs of improvement.

Florida Scott Maxwell, US writer
and playwright (1883–1979)

The children despise their parents
until the age of 40, when they
suddenly become just like them
– thus preserving the system.

Quentin Crewe, British writer on British upper class

Be kind to your kids, they'll be
choosing your nursing home.

Unknown

The first half of
our life is ruined by
our parents – and
the second half by
our children.

Clarence Darrow, US lawyer, speaker
and writer (1857–1938)

Thoughts on Death and Afterlife

Since I got to 80, I've started reading the Bible a lot more. It's kind of like cramming for my finals.

Vincent Watson

He's so old that when he orders
a three-minute egg, they ask
for the money up front.

Milton Berle

I used to hate weddings – all those
old dears poking me in the stomach
and saying 'You're next.' But they
stopped all that when I started
doing the same to them at funerals.

Gail Flynn

There are worse things in life than
death. Have you ever spent an
evening with an insurance salesman?

Woody Allen

I want to die young at
an advanced age.

Max Lerner, US journalist (1902–1992)

———

I've already lived about 20 years
longer than my life expectancy at the
time I was born. That's a source of
annoyance to a great many people.

Ronald Reagan

———

In Liverpool, the difference
between a funeral and a
wedding is one less drunk.

Paul O'Grady

———

If you die in an elevator, be
sure to push the Up button.

Sam Levenson, US writer and comedian (1911–1980)

Errol Flynn died on a 70-foot
yacht with a 17-year-old girl. My
husband's always wanted to go
that way, but he's going to settle
for a 17-footer and a 70-year-old.

Mrs Walter Cronkite, wife of retired US journalist

Memorial services are the cocktail
parties of the geriatric set.

Harold Macmillan, former British
prime minister (1894–1986)

When I get in a taxi, the first
thing they say is, 'Hello Eric,
I thought you were dead.'

Eric Sykes, British comedy writer and actor

My grandmother was a very tough woman. She buried three husbands and two of which were just napping.

Rita Rudner

❧❦❧

I don't mind dying. Trouble is, you feel so bloody stiff the next day.

George Axelrod, US screenwriter, producer and playwright (1922–2003)

❧❦❧

I know I can't cheat death, but I can cheat old age.

Darwin Deason, US businessman

An old lady came into the chemist and asked for a bottle of euthanasia. I didn't say anything. I just handed her a bottle of Echinacea.

Lydia Berryman

———

A stockbroker urged me to buy a stock that would triple its value every year. I told him, 'At my age, I don't even buy green bananas.'

Claude D. Pepper, US politician and spokesman for liberalism and the elderly (1900–1989)

———

My old mam reads the obituary page everyday but she could never understand how people always die in alphabetical order.

Frank Carson, Irish comedian and actor

THOUGHTS ON DEATH AND AFTERLIFE

Death is life's way of telling
you you're fired.

R. Geis

❖

I don't believe in afterlife, although I
am bringing a change of underwear.

Woody Allen

❖

They say such nice things about
people at their funerals that it
makes me sad that I'm going to
miss mine by just a few days.

Garrison Kiellor, US writer and broadcaster

❖

No one is so old as to think he
cannot live one more year.

Cicero, Roman orator and philosopher (106–43)

I am ready to meet my Maker.
Whether my Maker is ready
for the ordeal of meeting
me is another matter.

Winston Churchill

Life insurance is a weird concept.
You really don't get anything for it.
It works like this: you pay me money
and when you die, I'll pay you money.

Bill Kirchenbauer, Austrian-born US comedian

We think he's dead, but
we're afraid to ask.

Anonymous Committee Member, of the 79-year-old
Chairman of House Committee, Washington, 1984

All my friends are dead. They're
all in heaven now and they're all up
there mingling with one another. By
now, they are starting to wonder if I
might have gone to the other place.

Teresa Platt, US businesswoman

The ageing process is not gradual
or gentle. It rushes up, pushes you
over and runs off laughing. Dying is
a matter of slapstick and prat falls.

John Mortimer

Old age is like waiting in
the departure lounge of life.
Fortunately, we are in England
and the train is bound to be late.

Milton Shulman, Canadian writer
and drama critic (1913–2004)

If you think nobody cares whether
you are alive or dead, try missing
a couple of car payments.

Ann Landers, US advice columnist (1918–2002)

Women and Men

Trouble is, by the time you can read a girl like a book, your library card has expired.

Milton Berle

Few women admit their age.
Few men act theirs.

Unknown

Δn archaeologist is the best
husband a woman can have.
The older she gets the more
interested he is in her.

Agatha Christie

When women enter middle
age, it gives men a pause.

Unknown

The best years of a woman's life
– the ten years between 39 and 40.

Unknown

❦

Women are not forgiven for
ageing. Robert Redford's lines of
distinction are my old-age wrinkles.

Jane Fonda, US actress

❦

The lovely thing about being
40 is that you can appreciate
25 year-old men.

Colleen McCullough, Australian
writer and neuroscientist

My husband's idea of a good
night out is a good night in.

**Maureen Lipman CBE, British film, theatre and
television actress, columnist and comedienne**

A woman's always younger
than a man of equal years.

**Elizabeth Barrett Browning, British
poet and feminist (1806–1861)**

A woman is as old as she
looks before breakfast.

Edgar Watson Howe

When I passed 40 I dropped
pretense, 'cause men like
women who got some sense.

Maya Angelou, US poet, memoirist and actress

Whatever you may look like, marry
a man your own age – as your
beauty fades, so will his eyesight.

Phyllis Diller

❧—•—❧

The best way to get a husband
to do anything is to suggest
that he is too old to do it.

Felicity Parker

❧—•—❧

Age to women is like
Kryptonite to Superman.

Kathy Lette, Australian writer

Youth v Old Age

The old begin to
complain of the
conduct of the young
when they themselves
are no longer able to
set a bad example.

François de la Rochefoucauld

An old timer is one who remembers
when we counted our blessings
instead of our calories.

Unknown

I am not young enough
to know everything.

Oscar Wilde

Youth is a wonderful thing. What
a crime to waste it on children.

George Bernard Shaw

A man has reached middle age
when he is warned to slow down by
his doctor instead of the police.

Unknown

I have now gotten to the age
when I must prove that I'm just
as good as I never was.

Rex Harrison, British actor (1908–1990)

Old age realises the dreams
of youth: look at Dean Swift;
in his youth he built an asylum
for the insane, in his old age
he was himself an inmate.

Soren Kierkegaard

Young men want to be faithful,
and are not; old men want to
be faithless, and cannot.

Oscar Wilde

Twenty-four years ago, Madam,
I was incredibly handsome. The
remains of it are still visible through
the rift of time. I was so handsome
that women became spellbound when
I came into view. In San Francisco,
in rainy seasons, I was frequently
mistaken for a cloudless day.

Mark Twain

I never dared to be radical when
young for fear it would make
me conservative when old.

Robert Frost

The elderly don't drive that
badly; they're just the only ones
with time to do the speed limit.

Jason Love, US comedy writer

In youth we tend to look forward;
in old age we tend to look back; in
middle age we tend to look worried.

Unknown

Young people don't know
what age is, and old people
forget what youth was.

Irish proverb

The young man knows the rules but
the old man knows the exceptions.

Oliver Wendell Holmes, US physician, writer
and Harvard professor (1809–1894)

In youth, we ran into difficulties,
in old age difficulties run into us.

Josh Billings, pen name of US humorist
Henry Wheeler Shaw (1818–1885)

I have everything I had 20 years
ago, only it's all a little bit lower.

Gypsy Rose Lee, US actress and
burlesque entertainer (1911–1970)

In youth the days are short and the
years are long; in old age the years
are short and the days are long.

Nikita Ivanovich Panin, Russian
statesman (1718–1783)

The old age of an eagle is better
than the youth of a sparrow.

Proverb

In some ways, I never outgrew
my adolescence. I wake up in the
morning and think, 'Oh my God,
I'm late for a math test!' But then
I say, 'Wait a minute. I'm 40.'

Daniel Clowes, US author, screenwriter and cartoonist

One of the many things nobody ever tells you about middle age is that it's a nice change from being young.

William Feather

From the earliest times the old have rubbed it into the young that they are wiser than they, and before the young had discovered what nonsense this was they were old too, and it profited them to carry on the imposture.

Somerset Maugham, British playwright and novelist (1874–1965)

The old believe everything; the middle-aged suspect everything; the young know everything.

Oscar Wilde

Youth would be an ideal state
if it came a little later in life.

Herbert Asquith, Earl of Oxford and Asquith,
British prime minister (1852–1928)

Age is not different from earlier
life as long as you're sitting down.

Malcolm Cowley

People want you to be like
you were in 1969. They want
you to be, because otherwise
their youth goes with you.

Mick Jagger, British rock musician

Boys will be boys and so will
a lot of middle-aged men.

Kin Hubbard, US humorist and writer (1868–1930)

Youth is when you're allowed to
stay up late on New Year's Eve.
Middle age is when you're forced to.

Bill Vaughn, US industry writer

———————

I am getting older in a country
where a major religion is
the Church of Acne.

Bill Cosby

———————

I used to dread getting older
because I thought I would not be
able to do all the things I wanted
to do, but now that I am older I
find that I don't want to do them.

Nancy Astor on her 80th birthday

One day a bachelor, the next a grampa. What is the secret of the trick? How did I get so old so quick?

Ogden Nash

—•—

When you are dissatisfied and would like to go back to your youth... Think of algebra.

Will Rogers